Presenting Powerfully

Ideas, Outlooks & Actions
for Empowering Presentations!

Debbie Lundberg

Copyright 2011 by Debbie Lundberg

Debbie Lundberg, inc.

PO Box 13248.

Tampa, FL 33681

ISBN: 978-0-578-07932-5

Third Edition

Cover design by Sue Nance.

With special thanks to Marcie Falco and Yvonne Woods, who edited with insights and keen eyes…as demonstrated in the proofing of this work.

Presenting Powerfully

Ideas, Outlooks & Actions
for Empowering Presentations!

Debbie Lundberg

To my loving, supportive, fun husband, Michael Lundberg, as well as my encouraging, successful, driven clients.

Thank you all for coming to see me present, and for inspiring me with your presentations as well!

Please enjoy…

"Our work is the presentation of our capabilities."

~ Edward Gibbon

(English Historian, 1737-1794)

Contents

GUARANTEE

I guarantee if you do absolutely nothing related to the *Presenting Powerfully*, nothing will change as a result of your having read this book…

100% guaranteed!

Introduction

The Optimist sees the glass as half full. The Pessimist deems the glass as half empty. The Realist suggests getting the right size glass. And, the Opportunist drinks in all that is in the glass!

When it comes to presenting publicly, where have you been; on the side of the Optimist, the Pessimist, the Realist, or the Opportunist?

Public speaking, and therefore, making presentations, consistently ranks high, if not the highest of fears for Americans on various lists each year. Oddly enough, people like to speak loudly and regularly on their phones and in restaurants (and even in restrooms), dress particular ways, drive with certain abandonment and they don't even realize they are, in fact, presenting themselves...in a peculiar public way, just not in a traditional presentation format, and surely not powerfully!

While I have written books on taking ownership of one's life and everyday etiquette, this book is less about the day-to-day experiences of a conversation, and more about the less-than-daily occurrence of presenting in front of groups.

This book is designed for the Pessimist or the Realist when it comes to presentations and public speaking...with a huge dose of the Optimist sprinkled throughout....all with the goal that the Opportunist in each of us will apply all that will empower the inner presenter!

This book came about after individual clients, groups and corporate clients requested tips on talks, support for speeches, and overall presentation prowess. After years of those engagements, and realizing many people had similar questions and concerns, and even fears, I began recording the tips to compile into a digest for resource, reference and refresh throughout someone's occasional opportunity to entertain, educate, or persuade to a group of any size.

Now you have *Presenting Powerfully* in your hands. Congratulations to you! You want to improve the way you present, your presentation skills, your public speaking, and therefore you want to engage and direct your powerful self to present well. You are to be commended for your interest, and once you take action, you will reap the rewards!

It's likely you are far better at presenting than you know or believe! It's my experience that most people are. Sadly, though, there are a select few who truly see themselves as presentation gurus, so to speak, and their center stage impact is best left "back stage"! Hoping you are the former and not the latter in the aforementioned options, let's proceed...

This book is for people who are not attempting to be professional presenters, rather for individuals who are professionals who make presentations. What is the difference? If I were to write for professional presenters, some of the many chapters would read something like "Your Wow Factor", "Finding Your Niche", and "How to Brand Your Presentations". For professionals, like you, who want to make powerful presentations, those insights would be of less value and/or interest. And, I want to keep your interest and provide value! Likewise, this book will not delve into the art and science of Advertising or Public Relations, as those have a lot to do with presenting, but not the kinds of presentations about which this publication is addressing. So, in this book, there will be none of those "presenting for a paycheck" type topics covered.

Instead, please expect to get all the tips, tools and types of approaches for the presentations that will enhance and truly highlight you powerfully in the pages that follow.

In each of the 10 chapters, you will have a quotation to ponder, a Lundberg*ism* (a thought of mine from my talks, books, presentations, mental reflections and coaching), and then ideas and applications that directly address a portion or position regarding presenting...and they are brought to you for your use, your empowerment and your results!

"There are always three speeches, for every one you actually gave. The one you practiced, the one you gave, and the one you wish you gave."

~ Dale Carnegie

(American lecturer, author, 1888-1955)

LUNDBERG*ISM*

Mind the Gap between your expectations and your approach, and see the difference *in* you...as well as the difference *for* those following you!

Chapter 1

Three (Professional) Reasons to Speak Publicly/Present

While there may be many words, descriptions and even names for public speaking, there are three basic drivers, types, categories, or reasons for speaking publicly. They include:

- To Inspire/Entertain

- To Inform/Educate

- To Pitch/Sell

When you think Inspirational/Entertaining Talks, reflect or anticipate people who are typically telling a story, recalling an event, have a unique skill or experience, or are in a form of public service, a professional speaker, or a religious leader. Not all presentations in this category come from people who are titled as "Motivational Speakers", but often they do. My theory on "Motivational Speakers" is that while that is the title of many, it is not really the role of those speakers. Instead, the best title for those public speakers or presenters is "Inspirational Speaker" or "Entertainer". These titles would vary depending if the presentation were a recall of an experience (inspirational), or that of a humorist who tells funny stories (entertaining). Often these talks are thought of as "keynote" speaking engagements. Perhaps this presentation will start or end an event that spans days, will be part of a lunch or dinner where people pay to see the speaker, or it may be for a charity event where people are there for a mix of social, business and/or cause reasons.

This is the least common type of presentation most people will conduct. The majority of Americans will never be asked, expected or be put in a position to provide a fully inspirational/entertaining presentation...still, it is one of the three types. Providing you with insights about the successes and ideas that work in this arena just may push you to want to give a presentation in this format, or minimally incorporate some of the ideas in the other types of presentations.

For Informational/Educational Presentations, remember or picture teachers, cause/charity leaders, potential trainers, authors who talk about how to write a book, chefs who share the top 10 ways to stock your kitchen, and/or people who are engaged in certain roles with groups of children in sports or other activities. The realm of informing and educating is often taken for granted, and therefore, the preparedness lacks, and some people wrongly think because they are good at what they do, they will be good at telling people about it! That will not be you. You will be reminded that preparation and passion (even short-lived passion for a concept) are both key to informing/educating.

For most of us, this is either the most common or second most common type of public speaking and presenting we will do. Quite commonly these talks are given as "training" within a company or for a group. It is fair to recall somewhere you have been where there were many "speakers", and choices of presentations to see/experience for informational and educational purposes (at least that is what they were supposed to be there for!). Remember, though, few of us were awakened with the thought that we'd like to be "taught" or "trained" today (but many of us really do enjoy *learning*) so stick with informing and educating for what others can learn. With the learning perspective at the core of your purpose, you will be fulfilling a big part of the role of presenting powerfully in this genre of public speaking.

What may come to mind quite quickly regarding presentations that seem consistent in most people's lives are those related to sales, or perhaps more clearly, buying and selling. Some of the most memorable and lasting pitches, or sales proposals recorded and noted in recent American history, are those of the first "pitch men" from the Atlantic City boardwalk. Today, people at the mall, at our offices, and (far less than in the past, but still some) at our front doors, do attempt to pitch or make sales proposals to us. This is a type of presentation that will likely vary the most in venue and even audience, but will still be our most popular or second most in-demand type of presentation that we will either intentionally seek to master or be asked to master.

Interestingly enough, for an effective business presentation, which I suspect is the primary driver for most people choosing to read this book, often a combination of all three types of reasons is what will yield the most lasting and empowering results! For the purposes of this book, moving forward, unless noted, the chapters that follow apply to each presentation type, and all combinations of those types, unless clearly noted.

Having stated that, before you even shift into the preparation mindset for your presentation, first determine the reason you will be presenting. Ask yourself, "Am I charged to inspire/entertain, inform/educate, or pitch/sell?" Once the primary reason is clear to you, prioritize the three reasons: 1, 2, 3 in your mind, say them out loud, and record them on a piece of paper (or in a document). This is a process of connecting to your objective(s). If you think it, say it, and write it, your senses are engaged, and you are more likely to follow through on your plan. Also, knowing you want to be effective, and therefore include all three aspects, you will be less likely to overlook a portion of the reasoning as you prepare to present powerfully!

"Courage is what it takes to stand up and speak; courage is also what it takes to sit down and listen."

~ Winston Churchill

(British Politician & Statesman, 1874 -1965)

LUNDBERG*ISM*

Think and speak of things you *"want to"* get done, and you will do those things out of *desire and enthusiasm* versus what you "have to" do or "should" do, as that language drives a sense of guilt, burden or obligation.

Chapter 2

Six Parts to an Effective Presentation

Like a specific dance, a score of music, or plays for a sports team, people can learn the standard moves, or improvise, but regardless of the venue, regularly following the steps in the planned order proves to be the most favorable approach. The same is true for presenting powerfully.

The parts for which to prepare in your talk, training or pitch include:

1. Open

2. Preview

3. Body

4. Interaction

5. Summary

6. Close

The **Open** to a presentation may or may not include an introduction. (Introductions, whether or not to use them, and how to create them, are specifically covered in Chapter 6.) Regardless of how the words or screen appear prior to your moving onto the stage, standing up at your seat, or taking over the room in which you are presenting, you are "on". The way you open your presentation sets the tone for what follows. This is *your* time. This is about your audience, and this is when you can command a room, or leave people feeling like they want to demand to leave...it's up to you.

In the opening, you have a series of steps to cover as well, namely: a greeting to the audience, an introduction of yourself (if not given in an introduction), and the introduction of the topic you will be covering. Some people believe no presentation is good or effective without a story or joke at the beginning. I am a proponent of that for the majority of my presentations, and yet do not view that notion as a steadfast rule for every public speaker for presenting powerfully. I do, however, promote the idea of having something in your opening that is relevant to the audience and topic that you can also tie it back into the close for continuity and professionalism. Options for ways to open after you have greeted/thanked/acknowledged the audience, include:

- A visual on the screen or music playing (if you are using technology, which will be covered in Chapter 5)

- An activity that involves the entire audience

- An activity that involves only a few in the audience

- A statistic, study or fact

- A joke (if you are using intentional humor, which will be covered in Chapter 8)

- A short story (which could involve humor or not)

A visual on the screen or music playing has an element of surprise, and can evoke laughter, thought, or simply set the tone. Some popular approaches include a visual that has two perspectives for people to ponder, and/or a theme song (be careful, though, as technically, you will want to have permission to use anything presented as part of "your presentation").

An activity that involves the entire audience is something like asking everyone to respond to a question (yes/no questions are most effective), or each person to follow directions to see if the outcome is what is anticipated. Watch for the saboteur who may want you to fail from the start, or the untitled leader who may decide your activity is not worthwhile and "kill it" before it ever breathes life. Questions are a bit safer approach, and often equally as effective as an activity. Remember, if you are looking for yes replies, then lead in response with a resounding "yes!", and if you are seeking hands raised, be bold and intentional with raising your hand after saying "with a show of hands, how many of you..." when you are asking your question. Similarly, if you want people to stand to be recognized or participate/respond, use both of your hands outstretched in front of you with your palms facing up. With bent knees, raise your hands and your body to indicate an upward rising effort.

Strong personal confidence (covered in chapter 7) is the name of the game with activities. An activity that involves only a few might include asking a question of certain people/roles, or asking some people to come up to demonstrate something. The power of the few is that there are fewer chances someone will not participate, but the off-putting aspect is that some people may feel left out. If you select a small group, keep inclusion (versus exclusion) at the forefront. A lot of times asking for "the first six people to the front", or for "people who were born in certain states" is safe and fair, as those inclusions show no preference or arouse no offense typically. With these approaches, you simply get people involved, and can move onto proving your point and the activity for the audience to engage.

A statistic or fact is a useful opener since there is often shock value in it. The "Did you know…" approach is best when your fact or statistic is proven, you know the source, and likely the audience does not already know it. Asking "Did you know smoking can cause cancer?" is true, but common knowledge, where giving the staggering number of smoking-related cancers reported every day in the town where you are presenting, is compelling (as long as you are not there talking about fashion or selling cigarettes, that is!)! Facts and figures can sometimes be jarring. Leave time for a gasp or two in the audience or for people to process the information. If the "news" is unsettling for some, allow for discussion.

A joke is tempting, tricky, popular and dangerous…all at once. Chapter 8 will delve into much more information. Suffice it to say for now that you will want to really know your audience, know your delivery, and know that it is risky. Still, with risk can come reward. If you are presenting, your actual information may or may not be entertaining, so you will likely gain quick engagement and interest with an audience-appropriate joke.

A story is another option for an opening. With a story, you are demonstrating your relate-ability in a similar way you do with a joke. Telling a story does not usually involve as much risk/reward as selecting a joke does, *but it does hinge just as much on delivery.* Watch the message (not too deep or too much of an inside story or too much pop-culture-dependent). A story is about compelling people to follow your lead and buy into your approach, allowing you to bring it back at the end when delivered effectively.

Jokes and stories must be fairly brief (relative to your relationship and the amount of time allowed for the whole presentation), non-offensive, and pack a punch.

If any of your openings do not go the way you want them to go, the best approach is to move on. Let it go. If you belabor a visual, joke, statistic or story, it can appear as though you are pandering for acceptance. Rarely, and once you have really mastered presenting, you will be able to make a self-deprecating joke about the situation. I still rarely do, so use that approach sparingly, and use your smile and next point to move forward!

The **Preview** is where you let people know the agenda for the presentation time (not just the heart of the points of the talk, training or pitch). The preview is brief, but important because it allows you to fully set the stage for your presentation, take the lead, and keep things on track time-wise and for focus. A preview follows your opening, and it works well when you say something similar to: "Since we are here to discuss XYZ, let's please introduce ourselves, jump into the presentation, leave time for Q & A, and see where our next steps take us. By the end of the next 35 minutes, we will all have a better understanding of ABC. Let's get started!", or even "Often during similar events we cover X and Y, and the pace is up to you. Questions are welcomed, and throughout the interactive presentation, we will likely even touch on a bit of Z." This will lead to your actual presentation...with full engagement of the audience and direction from you!

The **Body** is the heart of the presentation. You may have read or heard that this is where you "tell them what you are going to tell them, tell them, and then tell them what you told them". That simple approach covers it, *but wait* (to borrow from those early "Pitch Men")...*there's more*...

The body includes a specific agenda which may include times (not recommended if your audience is filled with clock-watchers), and the presentation, itself. You may just speak to the points or provide a document with the information you are going to cover (handouts will be discussed in Chapter 4). The body of your presentation is where your energy and knowledge combine to fully inspire/entertain, educate/inform and/or pitch/sell.

The body is the formal presentation. This is where you "put your money where your mouth is", so to speak. If you picture a sandwich, think of the opening and close as the bread, and the body as the main ingredient (often the meat) of the sandwich. Other things, like the preview and the summary are like condiments or sides, and the interaction is the overall impact of the "meal" itself. Everything of value, consideration and convincing is to be included in the body.

In said body, be clear, stick to two to four main points you want to address or cover, and be confident in your delivery (confidence is addressed in Chapters 4 and 7). You will address questions during the presentation of the body, as well. (Questions will be specifically addressed in Chapter 8.) The heart of your presentation is where you demonstrate your expertise, lead the audience to reach a reasonable conclusion on their own...even though you are going to also summarize for them (and conclude the experience to a certain degree).

Interaction is less a step that *follows* sequentially, and more a step that *assists* all other steps in being successful! Interaction involves a lot of your style, attitude, approach (covered in Chapter 7), and the asking for business or compelling move to action (Chapter 9). Interaction is primarily about being there to create both a win and a want for the audience. Interaction is not just a win for you, or something you have as *the presenter*. Interaction begins long before the presentation (covered more in preparation in Chapter 4).

The more people with whom you interact positively, the more people who will want you to do well in your presentation. Interactions are everything from a hello and a handshake to a conversation prior to "going on stage" to the exchange during your presentation. Think of interactions as earning points with the audience or losing points with the audience. Each time your interaction is pleasant, or there is an "a-ha moment", your bank of connectivity with the listeners grows. But, each time you skip someone, present as disinterested, annoyed, are put off or off-putting, your bank diminishes. Sadly, the influx and exiting of the points does not happen at the same rate. For each interaction that does not go well, it takes 3-4 positive exchanges to "make up" for the misstep.

Interaction is the thread that holds the material together to create the project---the presentation in this case. Ensure your threads are woven often and tightly in order to keep the presentation and participants/audience tied to the topic, tied to you, and tied to the successful outcomes of the presentation! Remember that interaction is likely just as dependent on listening as it is on talking (reading the audience will be covered in Chapter 4).

The interaction does not stop when the **Summary** begins. As mentioned earlier, the interaction continues to be woven throughout every step. For the summary, this is a review of the entire engagement…from the open through the agenda, and is the set-up for the close. While the summary is often where people allow for Q & A, I already noted Q & A is encouraged throughout presentations that are not keynotes (this will be addressed in Chapter 8). A terrific way to roll into the summary from the presentation is to say something like: "So, as we look back over the past hour…", or "Imagine when we arrived today, we were not all on the same page regarding XYZ…". These examples are some of the ways to indicate to the audience that you have shifted gears without saying "In summary…", or "In review". The summary is not just a reminder of the points made (you did that in the "tell them what you told them" part of the body of the presentation). Formally, the summary is a recap of the entire engagement from start to finish (or near-finish where you will be from this point through the close). Take the audience back to the start with new words and quick reminders. Highlight the points of the body. Bring the message home in other ways and words while continuing the interaction and the interest consistently. A way to wrap the summary is to ask "Is there anything you wanted covered that was not?", and then wait. Silence is not *golden* in this case, but it is also not *deadly*. (More on this in Chapter 8.)

Once you have summarized, it is time to **Close**. The close is the tie-back to the beginning of your presentation. This could have been an opening question, a joke or some statistics or study, or even a story. In order to reconnect to it, begin with a comment, question or another statistic that brings the event/workshop/pitch/training full-circle. After all, you just summarized, and your continuity naturally guides you to the last word. The close is not simply "thank you". Yes, it is important to appreciate the opportunity to present. It is also not just a "that's it". While "thank you" alone is weak, "that's it" will absolutely deplete your interaction bank of connectivity. It shows only a sign of relief, lack of confidence, and utter disregard for the continuity in how you present. Plan for the close when you plan for the opening. (This will be discussed more in Presentation Preparedness in Chapter 4.) The close is your grand finale, it is the last request or last show of your fit for the business, so make it brief, lasting and compelling!

You now know, *or were reminded* of, the six parts to an effective presentation. They will not stand alone, rather in concert with one another. Much like dancers, musicians and team players, each aspect of the performance will impact the dance, the song, or the score, respectively. The same is true for presenting powerfully, and you want to present powerfully, so what would ever make you want to skip one or more of the steps? Nothing? Great, then onto avoiding mistakes and getting prepared!

"Anyone who has never made a mistake has never tried anything new."

~ Albert Einstein

(German-born theoretical physicist, 1879 -1955)

LUNDBERG*ISM*

If you are making progress, you're making some errors, but that's okay, you're also making strides, and no doubt, you are making *a difference*!

Chapter 3

Avoiding Common Presentation Mistakes

Things happen. Nothing's, and nobody's perfect. By being prepared (covered in Chapter 4), you will not avoid oddities and flukes, but you will hopefully avoid the top 10 presentation mistakes that most everyone (admittedly, author included) has made:

1. **Being uncomfortable, ill-prepared and/or not being well-versed in your topic.** You are there to be the expert, or at least an expert on the portions of the topic you are presenting! You may not know absolutely everything about a general topic, but know the few points you are covering, the angle you are taking, and/or the approach you are pitching. Get ready, and be appreciative and prepared to minimally get through the information successfully and with the believability that will warrant the respect an expert deserves.

2. **Alienating your audience and/or not reading our audience.** This can happen in many ways such as attempting to cover too much information. Pick 2-4 points, messages or highlights to cover, and stick with them consistently. Additionally, watch the attitude, the information, and your role as the presenter. If you come off as though you are "untouchable" or "above" the audience with too many points or a speed and depth that cannot be followed comfortably, you will lose the audience. Another way to lose your audience, and therefore, not recommended, is misreading or not attempting to read your audience. While you are presenting, the presentation (believe it or not) is about the audience, and not about you. Yes, stick with the plan and your preparation, but keep a pulse on the audience. For example, men, typically like statistics and graphs, brief

stories and short presentations, where women often enjoy stories and images, few studies, and will give you quite a bit of attention/time. If you have a mixed age and gender, level and education, keep that in mind and use an appropriate mix of approaches to your audience's interests.

3. **Complaining or repeatedly apologizing for anything**. Apologizing or anything more than once...being late (do not do it!), the room, technology, the food, the service, the handouts, your voice, "not being an expert"...*anything* is too much! If something is not your forte, then do not present on it before getting where you are the expert in the room. Have you ever been somewhere and heard "Well, I'm no expert", or "These slides are not the best, but..."? Any of those comments discount you, and discount your respect for the audience. If you have something happen that is not as you wanted it, either move on (if the audience doesn't know, there is no need to bring negative attention to it), or apologize once, and only once, and move on!

4. **Using technology and/or slides *as* your presentation instead of presenting with tools and support from technology.** You are the presenter, you may use tools to support and enhance your presentation, but the slides or videos, games, etc. are not the presentation. Bury people in the audience in flash and "the latest and greatest", and you will likely bury your message as well.

5. **Speaking to the screen, or too low for the audience to hear.** Speak to the audience, with eye contact (your style will be covered in Chapter 7) not to the screen. Use a tone and volume that is welcoming, commanding and at a level that can be heard in the back of the room.

6. **Using tools or handouts that are not the right size or readily available.** If you have handouts (which will be covered in Chapters 4 and 7), then decide if you want to *distribute* (never "pass out", as it implies you are about to faint!) them before or during the presentation. If you decide to distribute them prior to presenting, keep them in order, and consider having them face down until you want people to read them (human nature is to read ahead, which means the audience is not listening to you or seeing what you are presenting at the time). If you are confident enough to distribute materials during the presentation, have them where you can get to them quickly and get them into the hands of the audience efficiently. Also ensure anything you use as a visual aid is legible and clear to everyone in the audience.

7. **Using "verbal crutches" such as "um", "you know", "you know what I mean", "like".** It is better to say nothing. A pause can be empowering...let it be. Additionally "does that make sense" implies the listener should be able to follow it, and that the onus is on the listener to figure the sense in it. Instead, asking in a humble tone "Does that follow?", "Was I clear?" or "Did I address that fully?" is kind, professional and effective. Other verbal crutches you may have used in the past are: "and so on", "and so forth", and/or "and such". These are quite similar to using etcetera a lot. They do not add fact, form or any additional leverage/credibility to a statement. If there is more to add, just add it quickly and professionally.

8. **Mishandling questions.** Tell people how long you have if you are in the formal Q & A portion or your presentation. If you are not there, attempt to answer the question(s) without getting too far off topic. Having a "parking lot" (in concept, or literally on a flip chart that is titled "Parking Lot", or on

your iPad or laptop) that you introduce at the beginning of your presentation can keep you from rushing or going too in-depth. Whenever you have an inquiry, repeating a question assists the asker and the other audience members in following the flow. Additionally, while it seems supportive and positive to say "that's a great question", it is neither supportive nor positive. How so? Unless you say every question is "great", then it implies that the others are not so great, and may subtly discourage questions. Just leave out the qualifier, and state something before you answer like "thank you for asking", or "that is a question I rarely get". More to follow in Chapter 8!

9. **Being uncomfortable with a little bit of silence.** A thoughtful hesitation, and letting people think in response to a question you have are both signs of confidence in yourself and appreciation for the audience.

10. **Using your time poorly.** Presenters starting late, going over on time, rushing the Q & A, and/or ignoring the fact that other presenters are going on after that presentation, are all mistakes that happen far too often. The audience's time is nearly as important as respecting their intelligence, position, and choice to be there.

Surely each of us will have other "opportunities to improve" in addition to these common mistakes to avoid. As mentioned, nothing (and nobody) is perfect. Let's go for improvement, and personal best while "missing" these "avoidable mistakes" during powerful presentations!

"Success depends upon previous preparation, and without such preparation there is sure to be failure."

~ Confucius

(Chinese teacher, philosopher, 551-479 BC)

LUNDBERG*ISM*

Focus on the burn of the sun and you'll feel the heat, see it for the glow it provides, and you can appreciate the light...

Similarly, look directly at a problem, and you risk getting stuck on the issue...look beyond the problem, and you will likely envision the solution.

Chapter 4

Presentation Preparedness

Your best defense against avoidable mistakes is a good offense. Preparing for your presentation sounds logical, direct and perhaps even easy, but parts of it are subjective, create an atmosphere of being able to "think on your feet", and ultimately, are *simple* concepts...*and simple does not necessarily equate to easy!*

The segments of preparation preparedness that will be covered shortly include your knowing:

1. The objective

2. The topic

3. The audience

4. The room/venue

5. The time allotted and the agenda

6. The competition

7. How to write the presentation

8. Practice, practice, practice

The Objective. The objective of the event, talk, pitch or training will be your overall guide to preparedness. If you think you know the objective, write it down. Then, once you have it down ask yourself, "And what else", and then ponder "and what else", and finally, to ensure you are at the root of the objective, let yourself explore "and what else" one more time. Sure, I'm being a little facetious, but let's face it, most of us don't dig as deeply as we can, and sometimes only scratch the surface in our exploration, and therefore, in our planning. Some great questions to pose to the organizer of the event are included here. Realizing you may not ask all of them, minimally, ask some of these:

- What is the objective of the event?

- What will a successful event yield?

- How will you know/measure the presentation's success?

- Are there any parts of the topic/presentation that are off-limits?

- What do you want to happen as a result of this presentation?

- What do you *not* want to happen as a result of this presentation?

- What is compelling about this topic right now?

- Has this issue/topic/proposal been explored before? If yes, what were the outcomes, and what is different now?

- I hear the topic/approach to this event is _____ (what you anticipate it is), am I correct?

- Who, if anyone else, will also be presenting? (This will come up again in the section on competition.)

Knowing the answers to those questions will put you on the path to know what to explore in regards to the topic, and put you in a position to the topic well. Still the difference in knowing someone is looking to get something done, provided or shared, *is not the end of the research.*

You want to ensure you brush up on your topic expertise regardless of how many times you have presented on it or about it, as it will keep you fresh and focused for the presentation that is your upcoming opportunity.

The Topic. Once you know what your topic is you can then assert yourself as the expert, or become the expert. Hopefully you already are the expert, and if that is not the case, you can become an expert before your engagement. It is my theory that people who attempt to speak on a topic fall into one of three categories: 1) s/he is someone with exposure 2) s/he is a person with experience or 3) s/he has true expertise. The only fully effective presenters are those who have *expertise*. When expertise is leading you, your expertise is also supporting you and with your expertise you not only demonstrate, inspire, space and/or sell someone on an idea or product, *you can compel them.*

The Audience. There is an unfortunate belief in our society that knowledge is power, when in fact, it is the application of knowledge that is powerful. In knowing your topic, it is imperative you not only know it's for you, you know it *for* your audience...and ultimately and ultimately how your presentation can/will benefit your audience.

If knowing your topic well is the key, then the lock you are hoping to open is the audience. As soon as you know about your presentation opportunity, ensure you are aware of:

- The number of people in attendance. This matters for the space, the timing, and the activities, as well as your mental preparation.

- The age, gender, role/position of the audience. *One size does not fit all.* People of different genders, generations, positions and perspectives are interested in different things. It's tempting to deliver the same talk, speech, training or pitch regardless of the audience, and that may seem to work well for you, mechanically as the presenter, but will yield different results for you overall...and *different* is not necessarily *good*!

- The reason people will be in your audience. Some people may serve as information-gatherers, others as the decision-maker(s), and still others somewhere in between. Know to whom you are speaking, offering ideas or pitching so you can address their reasons.

- The audience's position on your topic. Was your presentation a request, of interest, or an obligation? Have they looked forward to it or did they just stumble upon it? Do they want you to succeed or fail? Knowing where your audience "stands" with regard to you and your presentation will assist you with connection and rapport.

- What your audience wants to hear. Are there "pain points" that must be addressed? Then address them clearly. If there is something to answer or show, then answer or show it. In Chapter 8, questions will be covered, and through questioning (and your subsequent answers), you can usually ensure your audience gets to hear what they want!

- Objections your audience might have. Have they been through something similar before? Are there hesitations? Is there an eagerness that may cause them to buy-in too quickly and not get their questions answered? Are the objections real or imagined? Overcoming objections directly and through your credibility is essential if you want ultimate buy-in, repeat business, or referrals from you audience.

- What the audience will be wearing. No, this is *not about picturing them in their underwear*; rather it is about ensuring you "fit in". Alienating your audience upon entering the venue is something that is avoidable. Being part of the crowd, with a little edge of style, skill, knowledge, and/or presence is where you want to be.

- Who the decision-maker is, if your presentation is a pitch. While this was mentioned briefly in the reason people will be in your audience, it is worth calling out here as well. The decision-maker may not be the first to speak, the loudest, or even the highest ranking, so pay attention to who looks to whom, what the verbal and non-verbal indicators are. Heck, you can even ask!

Getting to know your audience will give you a perspective that will remind you of your objective as well as your approach, and wanting to know your audience will keep you interested and grounded during you presentations.

A way you can keep things in check while they are going in the right direction is through cultivating and embracing your "moxumility"™. I define "moxumility"™ as having the confidence to go for something...the moxie, and the humility to ask for assistance and information. You demonstrate this with smiles and strength as well as questions and concern.

The Room/Venue. When you do your preparation work, it is key to know the location where you will be speaking. The way to prepare for room/venue is by answering the following:

- Is it in an office, at a conference table, in a hotel or at a convention center?

- Is the room lighted well, filled with poles or dividers?

- How is the sound?

- Will you want to use a microphone or a podium? Are they available or should you provide them?

- Is the location conducive to technology, or more of a podium/lecture place?

- How will the tables or seating be arranged?

- Where will you be standing/speaking/presenting?

- Who is the contact for the room?

No room is perfect, but many are great. No location is horrible, but a few are a challenge. A room in a location with plenty of parking and great lighting with no obstructions arranged in a "U shape" for small gatherings, or with round tables with the front-facing side without chairs or audience members for a larger group would be the best-case scenario. Still, if a room is dark, small, or with obstacles, and situated classroom-style, get the tables positioned on an angle for connectivity, move the seats with bad views, open the drapes and press ahead. Regardless of where it is, or the condition it is in, you can overcome and/or appreciate it and work with it if you know ahead of time!

The Time Allotted and the Agenda. Speaking of time...an hour meeting does not mean you get to talk or present for an hour. An hour meeting may mean you meet everyone with introductions, someone else presents, you present, questions are asked, comments are made and you all leave. A one hour presentation is a one hour *presentation*.

Ask for clarity on the time of the gathering/event, and the presentation time allotted. You are encouraged to ask if that includes your introduction and Q & A (both covered in later chapters). For a one hour meeting, the presenter, speaker or salesperson, or representative usually has 40-45 minutes, including Q & A when all is said and done (meaning by the time people start late, welcome everyone, there are introductions by one or all of the speakers, people change places, technology is engaged, there is a wrap-up, and a close). One way to get this information is to ask, and another is to ask for an agenda. Getting an agenda from the organizer is a smart way to learn a lot about the session beforehand. If no agenda is available, you can always share your agenda with times to get "approval", which is a way of seeking buy-in to your approach and your timing. If you get resistance to your timing or agenda, heed the warning and make changes that will not compromise your character or position. This is *free coaching*, in effect, for your being successful presenting, so if it is a tweak to the times, the order, and anything else, and it's doable, be thankful and be quick in the updates.

The Competition. Something a lot of us may not like to think about, but does not mean it does not exist, is competition. There is competition whether you are a keynote, trainer, or product/service seller/presenter. Competition is healthy. I think of competition as "coopertition", meaning we can all cooperate and make room for our expertise where it fits. As you prepare to present, ask:

- Are you having other presenters? If so, whom, and on what topics?

- In what order am I presenting? (First and last are preferred by most, and I like last the best since it gives me a chance to hear everyone, and act as the wrap-up for a line of speakers. Also, the audience, if they are asking questions, gets more ideas on what to ask throughout each presentation, so the last presenter may get "grilled", but if it is about thoroughness, the additional questions lend themselves to last (at least) seeming to be most thorough.)

- How much time does each presenter have?

- Are there other competitors/presenters speaking on other days related to the same cause/event/request for bid/proposal?

- Are you continuing to seek other presenters? If so, what is your criteria? (If they do not have the criteria defined, offer to do that for the organizer. A survey, description, spreadsheet for him/her to use is useful for them, and often endears that person to you, as you provided a value-add.)

How to Write the Presentation. Once you know your objective, the topic, your audience, venue, time and competition, you can write your presentation.

Start with your objective, and your message (they are not the same). Your objective is what you want out of the presentation, and your message is what goes into your presentation itself. Your overriding message should have a clear benefit for the audience – compel them to each want to listen to you…and they will listen.

Since you are thinking like both a presenter and an audience member, you will be able to develop and structure the content of your presentation to serve both your desired outcome, and the expectations of the audience. Technology and humor will be covered later, but suffice it to say you will likely speak lower and faster than you "rehearse" your presentation, so keep that in mind. Write an outline in bullet-point format, then write sub bullets, and those will eventually become either your slides (Technology will be covered in the next chapter), or your tool for practice. Somewhere between your presentation writing and your actual presentation, you will want to continue to refine and redefine your points in order to make your message simple to explain and create an ease around accepting that message as well.

Practice, Practice, Practice. In our country, it is odd to think most of us believe that practice makes perfect, when in reality, perfection does not come from practice, rather permanence comes from practice, and intentional practice will yield an intended presentation.

Make time, and take the energy to conduct several "dry runs" before your actual presentation. Reading and re-reading the words or notes, by the way, is not a "dry run". That is pre-dry run planning. The dry runs come from actually dressing and getting in the mindset of the audience, the location, and you for that time. There are a lot of different options for you during your practice, and all of them should be timed, including:

- Rehearsing while you are standing

- Rehearsing in front of a mirror

- Being video taped

- Having a mock audience of friends, family, or co-workers listen

- Engaging a trusted confidant on the phone to hear the presentation (email slides if using them)

Effective delivery is a dialogue, and not a monologue.
Remember, this practice is not an attempt to memorize a
"speech", rather this is a time to get to know your material and
direct your passion so well that you would be able to deliver your
presentation "in your sleep" if you wanted to do so (and boy I
hope you have better things to dream about than one
presentation!!)! Also, know your material so well that you could
present without the electronic tool/enhancement/distraction such
as PowerPoint. Your credibility as a presenter, representative or
speaker hinges on your knowing the information, and your
presentation.

Be prepared for questions and know the answers. After your
mock presentation, each time, whether it is from your review or
that of others, ask:

- What went well?

- What could be improved?

- How long did the presentation last?

- What questions are there?

- What's next?

Once you have fairly, and repeatedly, reviewed your efforts
(tough for many of us, as we are often our own worst critic), go
back, and repeat the segments you did not present the way you
intended in order to improve. After a break, go back through the
entire presentation again until you feel like you would be
comfortable (and even proud) to have a recording of your
presentation posted to YouTube for the entire world to view!

A final note on preparation is regarding the 24-48 hours prior to your presentation. While the following suggestions may have nothing directly to do with practice, they have a lot to do with your outlook, and therefore, your effectiveness in harnessing your presentation power:

- Get a good night's sleep

- Have a mantra that you can repeat internally to "pump yourself up" before and during the presentation

- Workout to get the "kinks" out of your body

- Eat things that are kind to you

- Drink a lot of fluids

- Surround yourself with as many positive things and people as possible

- Give yourself a pep talk about the reasons your presentation will be powerful

More about the day of your presentation will be covered in Your Presentation Style in Chapter 7.

"Technology: No Place for Wimps!"

~ Scott Adams

(American Cartoonist, b.1957)

LUNDBERG*ISM*

Thinking leads to theories,

and actions yield results.

Chapter 5

Technology...To Use or Lose It?

Technology (and the use of technology) can be a double-edged sword. When technology is appropriate, works, and can be seen/comprehended by all in the audience, it is usually spectacular, and enhances a presentation. When technology is not appropriate, does not work, and cannot be seen/comprehended by all in the audience, it is usually disappointing at best, and presentation-crushing at worst.

For the purposes of this book, and this chapter in particular, the idea of technology includes all of the following, and specifics will be noted for reference:

- Projectors (LCD or other)

- PowerPoint

- Interactive Games or Q & A

- Microphones & hands-free remotes

- Lighting

- Internet sites and/or chats

- Webinars

- Podcasts

- Videos (used during the presentation, and taping of your presentation

- Music

Here are some straight-forward considerations for technology in presentations overall:

1. Know your audience (sound familiar?). What are they expecting in general? If they want a "talk", then technology such as videos, interactive voting, special effects, and even PowerPoint, may be too much. If they want a training session, unless it is about how to paint a car in a downdraft paint booth, where the venue is the paint booth (or something equally as hands-on), you will almost always enhance your presentation with some technology such as PowerPoint, interaction with websites or live chats, and/or videos. If you are competing or pitching for business, unless you are a technology company representative, watch leaning on technology too much, and attempt to use some unique or non-predictable approaches within technology that set you apart and assist in "selling" you and/or your product.

2. Know your strengths. If you are great with technology, then use it, but just not to a point where you lose your audience or to show off your technology talents, rather to enhance your message(s).

3. Be heard. If that means using a microphone and sound system, then use it. Sometimes, technology is not the answer. Speak up, out and more slowly than you think you need to speak (no technology required). Music may enhance attention-getting moments or points, but then again, it may screech, not work, be too low or too high in volume, and be a miss.

4. Be seen and/or have your presentation be seen. Lighting is part of technology, as there will likely be times it is more important for you to be seen, and other times where the slide points (if you choose to use slides) are best to be seen. Learn about the room's lighting (as discussed in Chapter 4) prior to going "on stage" so that if you want videos or certain photos or slides seen really well, you can adjust the lights when/where appropriate.

5. Use a consistent message, picture, theme for buy-in and recall. This can be done with or without technology, just do not let it get lost in the technology.

6. Use photos and graphics to enhance your presentation's appeal to the audience. While the photo/graphic is not meant to replace you or your words, the visual will tie together well with you, your message and your impact, when those photos and graphics are complementary. (Remember to ensure you have the right to use anything you opt to include. Clip Art keeps you "safe" if you are unsure of copyright, etc.)

7. Even if you use technology, don't rely too heavily on it. Technology may fail...you do not have to. (The exceptions are webinars, podcasts and videos. Ensure you test and re-test the technology, as the technology is such a part of your presentation, that using it is essential, and failure of the technology may be failure of the presentation.)

If you decide to use PowerPoint, the seemingly only, and surely most popular presentation tool, remember, when you have your information together:

• Chose your color/theme for dark on light or light on dark (preferred), and watch too many colors or colors that blend together

- Use a 6 X 6 or 4 X 4 (preferred) approach with no more than 6 bullets per slide, and no more than 6 words per bullet or 4 bullets per slide, and no more than 4 words per bullet, respectively

- Proof your visual aids for spelling mistakes!

- Remove as many slides as possible, and have no more than 2 slides/minute of your presentation

- Keep consistent in your approach, and minimally have:

  - An opening slide with your information and the title of the presentation

  - A slide with the objective/purpose/goal of the presentation (the reason the people are in attendance)

  - An agenda slide

  - Slides that follow the agenda referring back to it (as headings) and providing more information (in bullet format, preferably)

  - Informative slide titles, so if people get distracted, and they will (it's them, not you!), they can quickly re-engage

  - A consistent color/theme, font, and size approach (some flexibility is allowed here for font size for impact, but not for color/theme)

  - Visual interest, like graphs, pictures, rather than just numbers and words

  - A slide that recaps the purpose

  - A slide that recaps the agenda

  - A slide for Q & A

- A closing slide with the presentation title and your information and ways to connect

If you opt not to use slides for your presentation, resist the temptation to memorize a talk, or even to read it (regardless of the type of room set-up), rather use a small computer to prompt you or cards or notes. Memorized talks feel "canned", and often distractions such as a question or change in the expected venue or delivery space create an environment that is not conducive to relaying a powerful message.

If you do decide to use technology, keep the following in mind:

- Learn the technology well

- Speak to the audience and not the technology

- Incorporate the human side as well as the technical side of your message

- If the technology fails, act as though it is not a big deal (because it shouldn't be!)

Overusing technology is not encouraged, but using it in order to avoid getting "hung up" on your wording or attempting to recall a memorized "place" in your talk, is far better than being "stuck" without a reminder of what's next. Technology will never replace practice, knowledge of your subject, confidence, and/or enthusiasm when it comes to presenting powerfully.

Let technology enhance where appropriate, and leave it behind where it is not appropriate, for as John Tudor once said "Technology makes it possible for people to gain control over everything, except over technology!"

"Diligence in employments of less consequence is the most successful introduction to greater enterprises."

~ Samuel Johnson

(English Poet, Critic and Writer, 1709-1784)

__LUNDBERG*ISM*__

Practice what you promote!

(No *preaching* required!)

Chapter 6

The Art of Introductions

This is the shortest chapter in the book. There is a reason for that. Introductions should be brief. If you are a presenter, or you are introducing a speaker, please do not read the person's biography. Refuse to do it. Embrace simplicity or abandon the formal introduction fully.

Believe it or not, an engaging introduction can be an important part of a powerful presentation. And, a bad introduction is often a sad start to a presenter who has to first recover from the introduction, and second has to attempt to engage an audience after that recovery.

An effective introduction should be **REAL**, meaning the introducer *simply, and only* covers the:

Reason for the talk/presentation/training. Welcome people, and let them know what the topic is.

Examples of the importance of the topic. State 2-4 reasons someone will want to listen to the presentation.

Acknowledgement of the speaker's credentials and name. Share 2-4 relevant facts about the speaker that will enhance the presenter's credibility and pique the audience's interest. Clearly and confidently state the name of the speaker/presenter last, with a pause between the last comment and the first name and a quick pause between the presenter's first and last name.

Leading of the applause. As soon as you finish the presenter's name to the audience (which is done while facing the audience. You then turn to face the presenter as you start to applaud loudly and rapidly to indicate others can follow (and they will!).

An example of "keeping it REAL" for an effective introduction is:

Welcome to the Presenting Powerfully workshop (**R**)! It is important we learn to present confidently and professionally, learn tips and tools for connecting with the audience, and that we get our messages across effectively (**E**). Our speaker comes to us as a 6-time published author, former regional and national leader, and a member of the National Speakers Association. Please welcome your expert on presentation prowess, Debbie Lundberg (**A**). Applaud immediately (**L**).

Part of an introduction that comes into use in both promotional materials, emails, announcements and/or on the screen if the technology allows, is a bio photo. Make sure your bio photo is current (preferably within 6 months of the presentation date, or minimally within 24 months of it). A bad photo, or one that does not resemble you is distracting to an audience, as the visually-oriented audience members will be attempting to answer questions (internally, and therefore distracted from your presentation) like: When was that taken? How much weight has s/he gained/lost? Doesn't s/he speak a lot? Does s/he really think s/he looks like *that*? I encourage truth, integrity and enjoyment in presenting, so in effect, if your bio photo does not look like you, it is your first "lie" to the audience, and you put them in a position to question all your truths throughout.

Know that if someone is planning to introduce you, it is up to you to ensure it is a REAL introduction...by opting to provide the exact introduction or to review what the introducer is going to say...or, decide to skip it. If you are introducing someone else, keep it REAL, and watch how that introduction is welcomed, admired, and leads to the start of a positive environment and expectation for the speaker and the audience!

If there is no formal introduction, resist our "about me" information immediately at the start of your presentation. *Your "about me"* is not the opening! Get the audience's attention first, share some ground rules or the agenda, and then, if appropriate, talk a bit about you. If there are introductions, you go last to show humility, keep the pace, and wrap to a smooth transition to the next part of your presentation.

Here's a format for guiding you through a REAL introduction:

<u>REAL, Effective Introductions</u>

(Who is the audience today)_____

<u>Reason</u>   the audience is there and topic:

_____

<u>Examples</u> of what makes the topic important   :

_____

_____

_____

_____

<u>Acknowledge</u> the speaker's relevant credentials :

_____

_____

_____

_____

(Name of speaker)_____

<u>Lead</u> the applause!

"Many of us crucify ourselves between two thieves - regret for the past and fear of the future."

~ Fulton Oursler

American journalist, playwright, editor, 1893-1952

LUNDBERG*ISM*

Sell yourself from
the inside out…

after all, *Product
One is <u>You</u>*!

Chapter 7

Your Presentation Style

This is not a chapter about putting on an act while you are presenting, rather it is about being yourself and making all your strengths work for you (and improving any areas you'd like to see greater impact). This chapter is about style, and allowing your style to work for you...whether that has to do with fear, which will be addressed first, or simply your demeanor.

Public speaking, as mentioned in the introduction, is often noted as American's biggest fear. Public speaking is not to be feared; *revered*, perhaps, but not *feared*. Based on my research, there has never been a person who died of embarrassment or public speaking, so knowing eminent death does not await, you can move swiftly into presenting powerfully knowing your worst results might be awkwardness, and likely, with your tools in use, your results will be terrific!

So if there is a great fear of public speaking that exists in the United States of America, how do so many people face that fear, find the courage to overcome that fear, and even master that fear?

Or do they...

Remember, people never knew what you were going to say (unless you tell them you missed something or did not deliver a message the way you wanted to deliver it).

Are there those among us who are fearless when it comes to public speaking? Perhaps there are. I believe in a concept I coined/created when I used to skydive a lot for pleasure called being "scared aware". This is the idea that you are scared enough to know you have fear, and yet aware enough to know your surroundings and have your wits about you. You can get to the point of being scared aware by acknowledging your fear or your perception of what is making you scared at that moment, and then walk through in your mind what could happen, what will likely happen, and what you can control within those "happenings". From there, the awareness becomes a preparation for what is about to take place, and in that preparedness, there is direction, focus, and eventually some calm (even if it is ever so slight). Fear only lives where fear is allowed life. Take away the life in fear, which primarily stems from the unknown, and the fear subsides...or becomes a much more agreeable companion: *nerves*.

I believe it is more about nerves and nervousness where people falter in presenting. Being fearful can be energizing when the fear is faced, and even harnessed. How do you harness that fear? When do nerves become empowering? How can we be courageous in our presenting?

Mark Twain said "Courage is resistance to fear, mastery of fear, not absence of fear."

The real question is what is FEAR? The way I like to address FEAR is by *Facing Each Apparent Resistance.*

I bring up the topic of fear again not to scare anyone, rather to remind each of us that FEAR is primarily the lack of facts or information. When you really look at what is concerning or bothering you, often it is not a fear, rather a discomfort, or anticipation of a future occurrence based on a previous experience. That is not to say your FEAR is not legitimate, rather it is to assist you in overcoming the situation. By addressing everything as an individual concern or sticking point, they can be addressed and put behind you.

Decisions about anything important, which includes your presentation decisions, are decisions worthy of gathering FACTS, worthy of gathering information. I like to think of FACTS as *Finding Available Considerations That Show*. In other words, FACTS allow you the courage to resist, and master your fearful side. FACTS replace fear by providing information that you can consider to shed light on, or show you how to be embrace them, and yield your courage and your confidence. Moving through fear, and allowing nervousness to energize rather than paralyze will empower you to embrace the nerves instead of "fighting" them.

Whether you have experienced seemingly overwhelming fear or nerves, your confidence will come from your interest, your preparedness, and your handling of the situation. Confidence will also likely come with time, but with time being of the essence, let's tackle what you can impact and own yourself through your **DEMEANOR**:

Deciding you believe in you. After all the audience wants you to succeed, and whoever hired or asked you to speak believes you are a great choice.

Eye Contact. Look at the audience. Let the audience know you want to see them. Being connected through your eyes will give you insight (no pun intended), and eventually calm you through that feedback. Stay engaged with one person through a full thought/sentence in order not to look jumpy. Do not look over the crowd, as many early public speaking instructional suggested. People can tell you are not making eye-contact, and either judge you as 1) aloof, or 2) scared...neither of which are good for you! Move on from one person after a thought is completed, so as not to appear you are having a personal conversation, and/or that you are alienating everyone else. Additionally, you want to move on to include everyone in the audience and never give one person the stalker-effect where you keep hanging on them throughout a full segment or talk.

Work eye contact in reverse if someone is being disruptive or talking with someone during your presentation. Resist the "dagger eyes", and instead, move close to the disruptive audience member without eye contact or comment...even sit on the table where the person is acting out, and watch/hear how the disturbance will be softened or stifled, without a word or becoming the "school marm" asking for silence.

Managing the Room. Talk with others as you check out the space. Walk around during your presentation. Make sure everyone can hear your voice. By stating something like "I take it you are assertive/professional/bold (your choice) enough in the back to let me know if you cannot hear me. I like that about you!" shows that "moxumility"™ again by showing the moxie to mention it and the humility to offer a solution. It's even better than asking people sitting in the back "Can you hear me in the back?" If you are comfortable with your materials and your projection, you may want to lower the volume to draw people in, and then raise the volume to make key points and show emphasis.

As long as you can picture, feel and hear your voice filling the space and the minds of the audience, you can do it!

Enthusiasm. Being enthusiastic does not mean you have to be loud; nor does it mean you should be loud. Enthusiasm is a confidence in you and your topic, a respect for yourself and your audience, and an energy that exudes from you that can be read...and even be contagious! A smile and sincerity are your two best assets in showing enthusiasm, and allowing others to appreciate your style. People follow sound and motion, and this is not to be confused with motion and noise. Remember, no giggle, no wiggle, stay enthusiastic, stay engaging!

Appreciate your opportunity to speak. Acknowledging your excitement/enthusiasm is not only okay, it is encouraged. Being too laid back can present as cockiness instead of calm. Say something like "Thank you for including me". Be sincerely appreciative of your opportunity. People want others they connect with to do well.

Normalize your situation. Eat well, be rested, wear what is appropriate, comfortable, and is true to the audience, activity and you. Have a mantra for your mental calmness. (I use my personal brand sometimes, and other times I simply repeat *"You are engaged, you are engaging, they deserve the best you!"*) Whatever you connect with that is a fit for repeating internally that is positive and focused, is a healthy mantra for you.

Offer intonation in your voice and movement in your presentation. Pace and tone changes that are not too wishy-washy or high pitched both offer variety, and therefore keep people's attention.

Relax yourself naturally. Meet a lot of people prior to going into the room or up on stage. Be "that person" who is welcoming, friendly, and approachable. Breathe deeply before going "on". Keep breathing intentionally and deeply (watch the noise if you have a lavaliere microphone!!) to keep your voice and pace in control. Have room temperature water close at hand, and ensure you hit the restroom before your presentation (one, to go to the bathroom, and two, to check your appearance).

Your DEMEANOR is your style. Let your demeanor convey your nerves as confidence, and your eagerness as energy, and let your passion for your presentation wow the audience in a way that is respectful, rewarding, and warrants a terrific response!

Presentation style is unique to you. While some things are not to be ignored or avoided, you can be true to you and the audience in your style. By ensuring you know yourself, know the audience, and know the way not only to manage a room or situation, but lead a group of people through a presentation with interest, awareness, respect and flow, you will keep your style points high and your results growing!

"Never treat your audience as customers, always as partners."

~Jimmy Stewart

(American Actor 1908-1997)

LUNDBERG*ISM*

People will follow your lead long before they will follow your words, buy your product, or promote your service...

Chapter 8

Engagement & Questions

Once your presentation style is really "your style", you have many other options, considerations and opportunities to engage, connect and survey your audience.

Audience engagement is something you cannot fake, force or manipulate. You can, however, create, encourage, and coordinate it!

Some decisions to make related to engagement, connections and questions include:

1. Your body language and confidence

2. Whether or not to use humor

3. How to get the audience involved

4. Whether or not handouts are appropriate

5. How you can use questions to pique the audience's interest

6. The best way for you to handle questions and/or question-and-answer sessions

As simple as it may sound, if you do not appear confident, people will not have confidence in you. Engagement is a form of confidence shared between a speaker and his/her audience. Eye contact and dress have been mentioned, but a couple of physical indicators have not. How you stand matters. Stand with your feet about shoulder-width apart, with knees slightly bent when you are not moving about the room for a relaxed, yet sturdy look.

Similarly, you have to have earned some likability points in order to earn the right to get away with your hands on your hips. Hands in the pockets can work if your head is moved forward to listen, otherwise, that can seem too cavalier for men or women. Whether you are having a great or awful hair, dress, stomach, attitude day, nobody will know it unless you tell them, so stay confident and make the most of who and how you are while you are presenting and others will not likely notice whatever is oddly distracting you. I rarely say "never", but here goes...never say something like "I am not sure what I can add to this, but...", or "I'm not really the expert", or "If I can do this, anyone can", as they discount you, and put doubt in the audience's mind. These comments are not endearing, rather annoying (at best)! If you think self-deprecation will work for you, think again, and perhaps lean toward a different approach.

While humor is an approach, and is part of your preparedness and your style, it is in this chapter because humor will either endear or repel your audience. So, choose wisely, and either be bold with your decision or be done with humor all together. Any and everyone can get a laugh...we just don't want it to be at your expense or the expense of someone in your audience!

Humor comes in many forms, including: jokes, funny stories, and visuals. I believe the risk related to those options lives in that same order. Jokes are risky because you have to ensure they are not offensive, get the order right, and then deliver the punch line with the right emphasis, timing and zeal. Funny stories can be personal, about someone else, or about someone else positioned to sound like a story about you. While few stories will offend, getting the points right, and then delivering the "message" to get the "a-ha" with the right emphasis, timing and zeal are similar to telling a joke. There is less of a personal connection with the story than with the joke, and still more than with a cartoon or visual. Usually, a visual tells its own story, so while you get little credit for it, you also are the most distant from it, and can move on from it fairly fast. If you decide to use a joke, a story or a visual, keep a pulse on your audience, and either allow for the laughter and processing (if it works!), or move to your next slide or point quickly (if it does not get the response you hoped to get).

For any approaches to humor, practice, practice, practice, know your delivery, test the tale or picture on "real" critics who will give you honest feedback, and in most cases, resist prefacing them with "here's a joke/story/photo/visual for you now". Make the joke relevant, hold back on laughing at your own humor, and certainly ensure you have permission to use any visuals you include in your presentation.

Much research has shown that most of a message is delivered through nonverbal communication. Depending on the source, the general consensus is that:

- 7-8 % is conveyed through the words and/or content

- 37-38% is transmitted through the tone of voice and volume of speech

- 55-56% is delivered through non-verbal information, such as facial expressions, posture, hand gestures, and how you present/carry yourself

Keeping those statistics in mind, engagement of the audience has many facets. Make it easy and simple (not the same thing) for the audience to like you and follow you and your presentation. Things like chewing gum, having noisy jewelry and/or coins clanging around, and having ill-fitting clothes or accessories at which you are tugging, are all actions and distractions to avoid. For the full engagement, this is often done through:

- Asking questions for input (and really listening to the responses)

- Using some of that technology like electronic input devices (game-style)

- Small group activities

- Think and Share

- Sharing stories for impact (different than stories for humor)

- Using many visuals and few words on a screen

- Keeping a theme consistent

- Sticking with your agenda

- Taking questions during your presentation (unless it's a keynote). More on this later in the chapter.

- Standing so your slides, charts, graphs, etc., are able to be seen by everyone in the room.

- Speaking with your audience; meaning not talking to the screen or just "at" them

- Letting your words be heard and you be seen! Even if you are using a podium, move around where appropriate (keynotes may be an exception depending on the environment) instead of hiding behind a stand, prop or podium.

- Enjoying and showing enthusiasm and animation in your approach and communication.

Handouts are both a point of engagement and a non-verbal communication tool. Handouts, given at the appropriate time, can be useful. Handouts given too soon, or in too much mass, will be distracting from your presentation. Resist giving your PowerPoint slides as your only handouts. There are times when it is appropriate to share your slides. If you can narrow the points to a few slides, or, often better yet, a worksheet that can be used as a guide or fill-in-the-blank follow-along form of engagement, it would be better. If you are using handouts, have them distributed at the time when the handout will be used. If you have a worksheet, you can have it available at the seats at the beginning of your training (or even a keynote). Handouts are not usually used as part of a pitch. Depending on the configuration of the room and seating, make certain you have the handouts in an order that allows the distribution to be swift (as mentioned in Chapter 3).

Using handouts often ties into approachability and interaction. Part of that interaction includes questions. Being open to questions during your presentation is encouraged. When you instruct your audience to hold their questions until the end, you demonstrate inflexibility, a lack of confidence, and a lack of respect for your audience. As soon as any of us thinks of a question, we want to get an answer. You will likely lose people in that moment and possibly for the rest of the presentation. Remember, all questions are valid, and by not qualifying the questions with "Great question", you are not placing judgment on any of them...or anyone! Keep in mind the guidelines for questions including:

- Asking at the beginning of the presentation what audience members would like to be covered in the next X number of minutes/hours. Talk about audience involvement! (Optional, and not for all presentation types.)

- Repeating the question for everyone to hear (unless the room or gathering is so small everyone surely heard it).

- Having a piece of paper and pen, or white board and dry erase or large flip chart and markers available for noting questions, points and general interaction where you can record things for referring back to later, and follow-through (similar to the "parking lot" concept mentioned earlier in the book). This may be useful in your close.

- Thinking before responding – even if you know the answer. It is respectful, and you will avoid a hurried appearance and/or missed parts to the question.

- Responding with "yes, and" to any question about your ability to do something. "Yes, and" is borrowed from many child psychologists and impromptu-skilled actors, as it keeps things positive. I like to remind myself to listen *to "know"* rather than listen *for the "no"*!

- Asking something like "Did that address your question?", "Did I answer that fully?", or "Was that the information you were seeking?" after replying to ensure your audience member, or partner, is satisfied.

- Including a slide for Q & A. You could have "Questions and Answers" on the slide, or something even more audience-focused such as "What do you wish you heard that you did not hear about XYZ topic?"

- Remaining calm and professional while not getting off-track or distracted by the "pupil" who wants to "stump-the-teacher". You will likely have one...the "question bug" or someone who thinks s/he knows more than you. Simply acknowledge that person's expertise, and let the person know you'd like to get their card to talk off-line to learn all you can from them after you are able to cover the information you were asked to present.

- If you do not know the answer to a question, do not lie, fake it, or attempt to avoid the question. Be direct, and tell the audience member you do not know. Ask if anyone in the audience knows the answer (if they might), and if not, let the questioner know you will get back in touch after research. (Taking the person's business card is a good touch, too.) Then, do get back to that person with the answer (and incorporate it in your next presentation if appropriate).

While surveying and follow-through are both covered later in the book, feedback-style inquiries and questions are healthy at intermittent places in your presentation. All feedback is a gift. Be thankful. Resist defending what seems negative. Use my Breathe/Tilt/Smile (BTS) approach to anything (feedback especially) where you want to ensure you do not come across as defensive or upset. You first listen to the question or feedback, take a breath to Breathe calmness into you, Tilt your head to the side to appear more approachable, and Smile before responding. This BTS tool will keep you from *reacting* and allow you to *respond.*

How you handle the first question will be an indicator for whether or not other people will feel comfortable asking more questions of you.

Posing questions to the audience that are not trite or too pedestrian will gain interest and engagement as well. Questions at the start of a presentation or speaking engagement will get the audience clued into the idea that they are participants, and not just attendees. You can use humor or be direct in your questioning...that is up to you and your style. If you want people to respond with the gaming devices for input to be displayed on the screen, let them know verbally, and act out the motion, too. If you want a show of hands, raise your hand in the air to encourage the response. When you are soliciting verbal input, be patient. It's great to say "let's hear from three people about XYZ...who'll be first?" If nobody responds, I often look at my watch, use my BTS tool (Breathe/Tilt/Smile) before saying "I've got 48 more minutes" (or however long the presentation lasts), and typically audience members laugh. Silence and pauses were mentioned earlier in the book. This is the time to let silence be your friend and not rush to answer your own question. You can wait, and rephrase and wait again, but don't fill the space with words to "feel" like you are progressing. Have the confidence in your questions that you and the audience will progress naturally. When you do get an answer, resist jumping in and/or talking over the respondent, or implying something is different than it appears. Questions asked by the speaker should always be respectful and not typically be tricky. Carefully crafted questions that become a bit of a story or joke can work if you have established both rapport and trust with the audience.

Engagement and questions are parts of a presentation that you cannot predict, but you can manage the situations well based on your readiness, open-mindedness and eagerness to be engaged, connect and answer questions yourself. Be interested, informed and inquisitive, and watch the audience follow your lead...

"You create your opportunities by asking for them."

~ Shakti Gawain

(Author, Personal Development Pioneer, b. 1948)

LUNDBERG*ISM*

Nobody says "*no*" until you ask…

and, a lot of the time, they say "*yes*"!

Chapter 9

Asking for the Business/Buy-In

Nobody likes to "be sold", but most of us like to "buy"!

Before you ask for the business (if a formal pitch against competitors) or buy-in (if you are selling an idea, or seeking support from a group, team, leaders or others), ensure you have identified the decision-maker(s) and the influencers.

Identifying the decision-maker is sometimes quick and obvious...that person tells you. Other times, it is a bit tricky. For influencers, it is far more interesting, as influencers need not be titled, but may be, need not be vocal, but likely will be, and need not be aligned with the decision-maker, but could be.

Here are some questions to ask of your contact who is arranging the meeting or presentation or training (note: Not one of them is "Are you the decision-maker?"!!!):

- "Once you review (or approve) this ... who will participate with you in making the decision?" or, "What are all the steps you will take in the decision process?"

- "Would you like me to outreach to anyone else or copy other colleagues on my communication with you?"

- "What prompted the interest in this topic/initiative/product/engagement?"

- "Who is driving this activity related to the topic/initiative/product/training/engagement?"

- "What obstacles, if any, do you see in getting this done?" (Often the reply is "budget".)

- "What has been budgeted for this topic/initiative/product/training/engagement?"

- "Can you provide me with an org. chart?" or simply "Walk me through the organization as it relates to the attendees, please."

- "What am I missing or did I overlook something that you want me to know?"

Most of those questions will get you to appreciate the reasoning/need for the business, some to decision-maker(s) roles, and others to influencers (especially the inquiry about copying someone on things). Once you have the above mentioned information, you will move forward, and have the meeting/presentation. With the answers you received from the contact, keep your mind open to note:

- Names and titles in introductions (especially if you have an organizational chart).

- Who speaks first and who attempts to but does not get to go first. If that happens, the influencer is likely the second to speak. (Often the coordinator of the meeting will speak first to set the tone and clean up details, so it is not always the first person to speak who is the decision-maker).

- Who waits for whom, who sits where, who gets "watched" the most. If you develop rapport, have confidence in you and your presentation, you will be able to observe and pick up on the seemingly subtle communication (and lack thereof) in the room/space. Watch them watch each other, and be mindful

not to be too upset if they are not watching you all the time.
Your role is to interact, inform, train, coach, inspire, but not
to let ego interfere with their dynamic!

Remember, as mentioned earlier in the book, get all the
information on your competition. Offer to create/provide a
comparison tool (this puts yours as the front-runner immediately,
and you have first billing, and control, to a certain extent, on
what is asked in what fashion).

Once you have identified who will decide, and who will
influence, remember the reasons people do not buy and/or do not
buy-in. These reasons include the following, and you want to
avoid and/or overcome them:

- Poor professional appearance. You are your #1 product!
  They are sold on you first, so that is within your
  control...present professionally and appropriately for their
  environment. Bad breath, poor manners, ill-timed comments,
  lack of respect for the schedule, all reflect poorly on you,
  your product or pitch, message and overall presentation.

- Telling and not compelling. While you are the presenter,
  watch talking through the close, over people, with any sense
  of arrogance or tone that is not inviting.

- No connection or rapport. People want to respect people with
  whom they work, and feel as though that respect is
  reciprocated.

- Missing key details of the wants and needs of the
  client/potential client. Overlooking who is an influencer
  and/or a decision-maker is a sure way to get a quick and

insincere "Thanks for coming in. Don't call us, we'll call you."

- Attempting to be "all things to all people". You are not. I am not. Let's get real. If you are able to do things, then yes, and if not, it is a "yes, and that will require our working with a vendor in XYZ, which we can surely coordinate". If something or some time requested is not going to be met, be clear, because you can win the battle of the inquiry and lose the war of the repeat business with over-promising.

- Not closing fully and not asking for the business. Be bold and be appreciative. That "moxumility"™ is not going away as an attribute for a successful, effective, empowering presenter. Ask how you can "earn" the business. Let the audience know how much you want it, will work for it, appreciate the opportunity and look forward to living up to your promises!

A "test-the-water" confidence-building approach to presenting is to ask questions for buy-in throughout, and ask for yes/agreement. This is accomplished by making inquiries for both involvement/engagement, and a trial run on the buy-in. It is proven time and time again that small agreements received throughout a presentation or pitch will result in a more likely cumulative effect of a yes later. I like yes, applause or survey-result type questions as well as either-or options. Some examples are:

- "Yes, or no - Is this idea something you can see around here?"

- "By the noise meter of applause, indicate how close I am to hitting the target of what you want me to cover."

- "Using your keypads (if you are using that technology!), please vote for the style you like best." These will then display on the screen, you can note the results and discuss them. This will be a refer-back later in the actual close.

- "Do you like option A or Option B? Let's see hands for A...now hands for B." Then talk about the reasons.

Now it is time to really *ask for the business*! For a presentation to inspire/entertain, you are looking for appreciation, applause, and, possibly referrals. In an inform/train scenario, you are seeing applause, approval, and minimally that you met the objective of the time/session and that your audience is satisfied. In a pitch/sale meeting, you want an order, agreement and business partnership.

Sadly, strangely, and consistently, it has been estimated that 60-70% of sales that do not happen, do not come to fruition because the business was not asked for by the seller! Repeatedly sales are lost because the pitch person, sales representative, or product expert is uncomfortable about asking...mostly for fear of rejection.

Give yourself credit. By the "ask", if you have followed all the other steps and have been sincere, as outlined in this book, then closing the sale should be a natural progression in the conversation and presentation. Here are some examples:

- Ask what they see as next steps, and follow their lead with an opening to the closing process such as "Knowing we agreed (because you requested intermittent buy-in) I/My Company are capable to do the work and we would like to earn the contract, what are the appropriate next steps?". This is somewhat soft, and can be ambiguous. You hate to get "We'll call you." in response, but often the attendees/audience will openly and freely tell you more than you would expect.

- Ask for the objections (in a new way). This is bold, and yet fairly expected. If you say something similar to "Knowing all our capabilities, and that we want to earn your business, is there anything that would keep you from hiring/choosing us (or implementing the process if it is a training or even inspirational talk)?" Since you put it out there, you may hear many things the potential clients do not like. I appreciate that, though, since if you don't ask, they often will not disclose. This is not a sit-and-wait approach! You may even hear a "no, you are just not a good fit", and that can still keep the conversation going, or it could stop the process right there. Again, I believe you are better to know what is in the mix for the decision-making process than leaving with a "hope and pray" for the business attitude/approach.

- Ask for the business directly. Some approaches are as clear as "Can we rely on your business?", "When would you like to get started?", "How many shall we order for you?", or "Do you want me to go into the contract now?". Other ways to close here are setting up a meeting for the order, or a deadline for the number of items and quantities of each. You can incorporate those refer-back buy-in indicators mentioned above here for reinforcement and reminder of their interest. Just flat-out asking for the business can increase your sales dramatically and quickly. Most people miss this part!

- Ask for the referral. Sometimes it is not appropriate, but other times it is, so you'll assess if at the close of your presentation you can ask for a referral. This will be covered in Chapter 10 as well, as it is often done post-presentation. If you are asking for a referral while presenting, it is likely a train/inform session where you are asking if there is someone else, or another organization where this presentation would benefit. Be careful here, as nobody feels good about paying to be somewhere to learn something, and then getting any sense of pressure for other business. Do not do this if there is a risk that those present will feel undervalued at the end of the day/event. This has a lot to do with rapport and sense of the audience than simply having a slide or point to cover.

Once you get over the discomfort (if you had some) of asking for the next progression in the partnership, you will be glad to know where you stand and what to do. You are almost done, but not quite. You have asked for the business, and you ended your presentation. Still, you have not concluded fully. Whatever presentation type you are engaged in, show gratitude with a thank you, a smile, and great positioning and posture before you exit. Even if you do not get referrals, the business that day, or a standing ovation, be proud of yourself, and be grateful for their time and attention. You set the tone for their reflection based on how you exit. Let your exit be bold, be brief, and be about the audience, because even though you are leaving, there will still be "work" to do that relates to the presentation!

"Accept business only at a price permitting thoroughness. Then do a thorough job, regardless of cost to us."

~Arthur C. Nielsen

(Founder the AC Nielsen Company, 1897-1981)

LUNDBERG*ISM*

At the end of the day, when you rest your head on your pillow, you are the only one who knows if you gave your absolute best in all you did during your waking hours.

Chapter 10

The Presentation After the Presentation

Just when you thought it was done, your presentation is still going...in the form of follow-up, follow-through, and more wowing!

Some things to do/conduct after the formal part of your presentation are on-site and some are off-site, and they include:

- A survey

- A quick ask

- A business card exchange

- A drawing/give-away

- A vote

- A summary

- A thank you

- A follow-up plan

Survey. When you are in front of someone, or a group of people, that is the best time to act, and assess. A survey is very appropriate and typical in American culture. I suggest you give your survey at the beginning of the presentation to all attendees, and address it. Let the audience members know you want to earn the highest score (not get it). This ensures they know you are accountable to that survey. When you have the surveys, be thankful, and once you tabulate the results, regardless of what they are, ensure you report back what the scores and comments were (with more gratitude). Defend nothing, show appreciation, and even let people know answers to questions or how you will improve, if there were questions/suggestions.

Quick ask. Much like a survey, an "ask" is done with just one or two people. Think about asking "From your perspective, what went well?", as well as "What could be improved?" of one or two key individuals. If you have gained the confidence, and are really ready for it, ask "What would you and others say about me if I weren't in the room?" That is something few will ask, but for those who do, the question can be a Pandora's Box or a reinforcement of what you had hoped they would say. Either way, it gains a lot of credibility in the minds of the responders if you take the coaching/feedback well.

Business Card Exchange. A business card exchange is definitely a must at a pitch presentation to ensure you have contacts for contracts and future business. Similarly, for train/inform and entertain/inspire talks and presentations, there is potential to add people to your contact list, for networking, to include in your monthly newsletters (if you have permission within the exchange), and for later reference if they want to share theirs. For you, you want your image and powerful presentation impact to continue with your reference and contact, which, in our society, is a business card.

Drawing/Give-Away. In any type of presentation, there can be an appropriate and fun time for a give-away. These can be done with products you are promoting, books you have written, items or publications associated with your business or inspiration, and other things, too. Stick with something that fully connects the recipient to you, though, as I see a lot of gift cards and prizes with no affiliation to the presenter, and think of what a lost opportunity that is/was. Give-aways and drawings can be based on answering or asking questions, the business cards you have collected, and other creative approaches. Ensure there is not a cheesy factor or that you are giving the impression that your audience is being treated like trained seals. Keep it fun and professional while encouraging and rewarding the audience!

Vote. Whether or not you are using the voting technology mentioned earlier in the book, you still can take votes for input and/or prizes. Voting on ideas, proposals, or product ideas can really engage the audience, and give a preview of your potential, overall buy-in. You can even have votes for who contributed the most to a session or pitch, if you like...the possibilities are only limited by your creativity.

Summary. While you will summarize your presentation points during your presentation, you may also want to summarize the entire event at the event briefly and/or immediately following the event to all the attendees. This is terrific for the learning and exchange, and from a business perspective, it gives you a chance to show your powerful presentation and points in a new light. You can do a summary of the experience with the team, group, company, and your empowering points to show the connection to/with you and your business. Additionally, offering a post-presentation summary or two will keep people professionally connected to you and your value. This is done most easily if you collected business cards and received permission for communication rather than having one point of contact you are relying on to forward your communication or information.

Thank you. Similarly, a "thank you" done at the presentation is imperative. A "thank you" written to each attendee or leaders of groups, minimally, is something few people make time to do. Emails are nice, but a handwritten note with something included, like an article or book related to the presentation, makes a lasting impression.

Follow-Up Plan. While I am optimistic, I am realistic as well. Knowing that, be aware, you may not have gotten the business immediately, or the full response you wanted. Hopefully you did. Whatever response/result came immediately out of your presentation, have a follow-through plan for the attendees beyond what has already been mentioned, in the form of:

- Newsletters

- Weekly tips

- Mailings

- Calls to decision-makers

- Articles

- Invitations

Plan to be a partner with the attendees for a long time to come, and your presentation after the presentation will likely lead to more presentations, and more business.

A presentation is often only thought of as the formal "on stage" part of the interaction, but the follow-through becomes an extension of the great impression you made, or takes away from all your efforts...it's up to you.

"The two most engaging powers of an author are to make new things familiar, familiar things new."

~ William Makepeace Thackeray

(Indian-born Novelist of 'Vanity Fair', 1811-1863)

LUNDBERG*ISM*

Nobody's perfect.

Embrace the notion of *progress... not perfection* in order to keep learning and realizing results that can be measured and maximized!

Final Thoughts

Where are you now in the Optimist, Pessimist, Realist scenario in regards to public speaking and presenting? I continue to be the extreme Optimist who seeks out the Pessimists and Realists to engage and assist with empowering them and their presentations! Here's hoping you have found some ideas, approaches and actions for empowering your presentations.

It's a funny thing about guide books. Many get purchased, some get read, and few get implemented. As an author, that is encouraging and depressing all at once. Sure, it's terrific you bought (or someone bought) this book (for you), but what will you do now? If you have gotten this far in the publication, you are either really interested or a great skimmer and this line caught your eye. I hope it is the former over the latter, but nonetheless, it really is up to you.

Reading this book will not change the fact that we live in a culture, and perhaps inside a mind where public speaking is more feared and admired than so many other things. It is not that someone has to get good at presenting, rather presenting *powerfully*. Taking all the concepts into consideration, and many into action, will create a wonderful opportunity to stand up, stand out, and make an impact on the audience for a lasting impression, and perhaps long-standing results.

While there has been a lot of "advice" type language in this book, the comments are suggestions. The lists are optional for anyone...for everyone. Do you want to be part of the crowd, one of the statistics who "hate getting up in front of people", or do you want to be empowered by your implementation of the ideas in concert with your own natural abilities and learned skills?

Do I believe everyone has charisma? No. Do I believe each person can become an effective presenter? Yes. What is the difference, and how are they similar? Charismatic people often just draw people in. People like to follow, and seemingly naturally follow charismatic people. They are empowered with/by their charisma and how they utilize it. People who are effective presenters create a sense of expertise, and in effect a compelling reason to follow them, to draw people in. They are skilled and have learned the approach, and yet, they, too, are empowered. Most people do not fear being charismatic, and yet the public speaking and presenting challenges often paralyze or bring about envy in the way charisma does. The difference with charisma and effective presenters is that the presentation skills can be studied, learned and implemented.

Remember, though, if you have read this book, and you do agree to present, do it to the best of your ability. Keep in mind you will want to:

- Decide the type of presentation you are making

- Put together the six parts of your presentation

- Review the mistakes to avoid

- Get prepared

- Know your technology

- Ensure a REAL introduction, or none at all

- Be true to your presentation style and DEMEANOR

- Work toward engagement, connection & questions

- Ask for the business/buy-in

- Follow-through after the presentation

You know this. You are already successful in many ways. You believe you can be a powerful presenter. Michael Jordan said it best when he said "You miss 100% of the shots you never take". Take your shot. Make the time, take the steps, and reap the benefits of being empowered. Overcome that fear, or at least the fear of so many Americans, and be the person, whether you are an optimist, pessimist, realist, or opportunist, who presents powerfully!

Thank you for reading *Presenting Powerfully*!

If you would like more copies of this book, other Debbie Lundberg publications, or to have a workshop on *Presenting Powerfully*, please email Debbie@DebbieLundberg.com, or send your request to:

Debbie Lundberg Life & Business Coaching

PO Box 13248

Tampa, FL 33681

813.835.0196

Comments, ideas, success stories and/or questions are welcome at/through:

Debbie@DebbieLundberg.com

http://www.DebbieLundberg.com

http://www.ReversingTheSlobificationOfAmerica.com

http://DebbieLundberg.blogspot.com/

Facebook.com/DebbieLundbergLifeandBusinessCoaching

http://www.linkedin.com/in/DebbieLundberg

http://twitter.com/DebbieLundberg